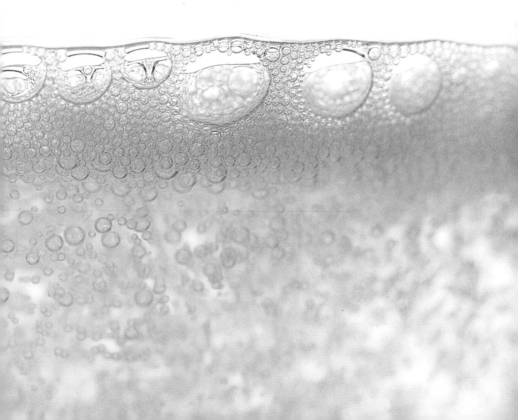

Bubly

Bubbly

Jonathan Ray

RYLAND
PETERS
& SMALL
London New York

First published in the United States in 2001
by Ryland Peters & Small, Inc.
519 Broadway, 5th Floor, New York NY 10012
www.rylandpeters.com

10 9 8 7 6 5 4 3 2
Text © Jonathan Ray 2001
Design and photographs
© Ryland Peters & Small 2001

Library of Congress Cataloging-in-Publication Data

Ray, Jonathan.
Bubbly / Jonathan Ray.
p. cm.
ISBN 1-84172-184-0
1. Champagne (Wine) I. Title.

TP555 .R43 2001
641.2'224--dc21   2001031620

ISBN 1 84172 184 0

Printed and bound
in China.

contents

what's all the fuss about fizz?

It may only be a glass of fermented grape juice with a few bubbles in it, but imagine how flat a celebration would be without fizz, champers, pop, or bubbly…

The term "sparkling wine" refers to any wine that contains bubbles of carbon dioxide, the most revered example of which is called champagne. Although in truth it is no more than this, bubbly is special: poems have

CELEBRATION!

been written about it, songs sung about it, and it is synonymous with celebrations and gaiety. It is inconceivable to think of acclaiming a newborn, commemorating a victory, or saluting the New Year without a bottle of bubbly. And what on earth would playboys sup from starlets' slippers other than frothsome fizz?

There is never a wrong time for a glass of bubbly: simply uncork a bottle and you immediately elevate a gathering into a party. Asked on what occasions she would take champagne, the late Madame Bollinger famously replied: "I drink it when I'm happy and when I'm sad. Sometimes I drink it when I'm alone. When I have company I consider it obligatory. I trifle with it if I'm not hungry and drink it when I am. Otherwise I never touch it—unless I'm thirsty."

just a little
bit of history

It doesn't do to make a big thing about it while in a room with French people, but there is some evidence to suggest that it was the British who invented champagne.

Up until the late 1600s the wine made in Champagne was flat. French glass was too weak to make bottles strong enough to contain sparkling wine, and cork stoppers were a thing of the future. The English, on the other hand, were already using cork stoppers in their bottles, as well as having perfected making glass strong enough to confine fizzy wine. There is also evidence that the English were in the habit of adding sugar to imported wines—notably those from Champagne—to

make them sparkle, some twenty years or so before the Champenois had figured out how to make their wine fizzy. On the other hand, there are those who claim that Blanquette de Limoux, a fine sparkler made in the south of France, predates sparkling champagne production by some 150 years. Wherever or however it was invented, it soon became apparent that the soil, climate, and choice of grapes in Champagne were ideal for the production of bubbly. Even though it is now made all over the world, from Argentina to England, from India to New Zealand, the only sparkling wine entitled to call itself champagne is that which is made in the region of

that name, using
no grapes other
than Chardonnay,
Pinot Meunier, and
Pinot Noir, by the
reputable Méthode
Champenoise.

The vineyards of the Champagne region are the most northerly in France, and the grapes have difficulty ripening fully, leaving them high in acidity and low in

SO GLAMOROUS!

flavor—ideal for winemakers seeking to achieve the austere, elegant style characteristic of the best champagnes. Unlike in the New World, biting frosts and hailstorms can affect the quality of each year's harvest dramatically, and as a result, 80% of production is devoted to non-vintage champagne.

Champagne comprises only a fraction of the total production of sparkling wine, but our fondness for it is clear, given that 320 million bottles are consumed around the world every year.

Although other sparkling wines might be made from such varieties as Chenin Blanc, Muscat, Müller-Thurgau, Aligoté, Clairette, Riesling, and Pinot Blanc, champagne may only be made from Chardonnay (sometimes used on its  own to make **blanc de blancs**) —and two red grapes, Pinot Noir (best-known for making red burgundy) and its close relative, Pinot Meunier, a grape little seen elsewhere, but highly prized here for adding fruit and acidity to the champagne blend. Despite being red grapes, these last two varieties are sometimes used without Chardonnay to make a white champagne (**blanc de noirs**).

why bubbly
is bubbly

Méthode Champenoise is the most successful process used to make wine fizzy. Most top-quality sparkling wines and all champagnes are produced this way.

Grapes are picked and pressed, and the resulting juice undergoes an initial fermentation—usually in stainless steel tanks—although some producers prefer to use oak barrels. Once fermented, the wines (which may be from different vintages, vineyards, and grapes) are blended together. Before bottling, an additional solution of yeast, sugar, and wine (**liqueur de tirage**) is added, causing a second fermentation in the bottle which produces the bubbles.

Sealed with crown caps, the bottles mature on their sides for up to three years, after which they are regularly turned and gradually tilted—or "riddled" (**remuage**)—until they are vertical, causing the sediment created during the second fermentation to fall into the neck of the bottle. The necks are frozen, and the icy pellet of sediment is expelled by removing the cap—the pressure of the fizzy wine forces the icy plug out (**dégorgement**). Prior to corking and labeling, a mixture of wine and sugar (**liqueur d'expédition**)

is introduced to the bottle (**dosage**). An alternative system that is often used to produce sparkling wines is known as the **Transfer Method**. Wines that have undergone their second fermentation in the bottle are disgorged under pressure into tanks—the whole contents, not just a frozen plug—prior to filtering and rebottling. This method is widely used in the New World and it produces very decent wines, albeit without the finesse and elegance of those made by the **Méthode Champenoise**. This is a much less expensive process since it removes the time-consuming "riddling" and the costly freezing, disgorging, and topping up of each bottle individually.

The **Tank Method**, also known as the **Cuve Close** or the **Charmat Process**, involves a second fermentation in a sealed tank instead of a bottle. Most German Sekt is made this way, and while it is good, it doesn't have such fine

MAKING THE BUBBLES

or long-lasting bubbles as wines that are made by the previous methods. **Carbonation** is the cheapest and least effective method of injecting bubbles into wine, via what the French jokingly refer to as a **pompe bicyclette**.

something
for everyone

Champagne commands a premium, sometimes unfairly. Without a doubt, a well-made sparkling wine from anywhere else is preferable to a poorly made champagne.

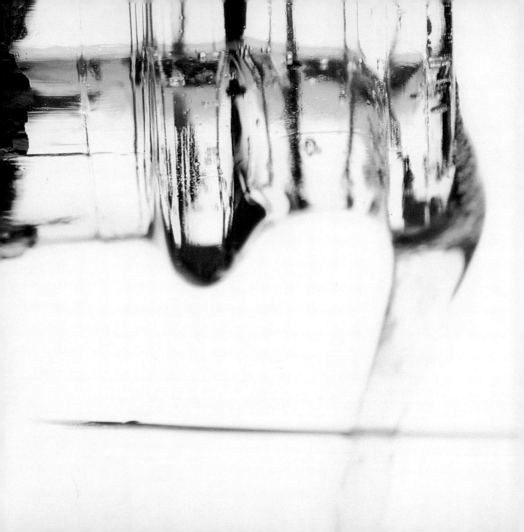

Champagne is generally marketed under brand names, among the best-known of which are Bollinger, Gosset, Jacquesson, Krug, Moët & Chandon, Mumm, Pol Roger, Louis Roederer, Ruinart, Salon, Taittinger, and Veuve Clicquot. The excellent bubbly

BIG NAME BUBBLES

made elsewhere in France does not have such high-profile brand names, although high-quality regional wines are well worth seeking out, such as Crémant d'Alsace, Crémant de Bourgogne from Burgundy, Blanquette de Limoux from Languedoc-Roussillon, sparkling Saumur and Vouvray from the Loire, and Clairette de Die from near Grenoble.

Other Old World bubbly includes Cava from Spain; Sekt from Germany; and Prosecco, Franciacorta; and the deliciously sweet Asti from Italy. But the biggest revolution in sparkling wine has occurred in the New World, with wonderful Méthode Champenoise bubbly now being produced including Quartet and Mumm Cuvée Napa from California, Pelorus from New Zealand and the Australian-made Seaview, and Taltarni. England's finest fizz is prize-winning Nyetimber. All worth a try!

From the huge photo-opportunity Nebuchadnezzars that require three or more people to lift them, to chic quarter-bottles drunk with a straw in trendy night-clubs, bubbly bottles are famous for their variety of sizes:

Quarter-bottle 20cl/200ml
Half-bottle 37.5cl/375ml
Bottle 75cl/750ml
Magnum 2 bottles
Jeroboam 4 bottles

Rehoboam 6 bottles
Methuselah 8 bottles
Salmanazar 12 bottles
Balthazar 16 bottles
Nebuchadnezzar 20 bottles

This short glossary might help make bubbly's terminology less confusing:

Blanc de blancs A white wine made solely from white grapes.
Blanc de noirs A white wine made solely from red grapes.
Brut Dry.
Crémant Wines that are only lightly sparkling.
Demi-sec Semisweet.
Doux Sweet.
Extra brut Very dry.
Extra dry Dry.

Extra Sec Dry.
Mousse The froth that fizzes in a glass of sparkling wine as it is poured.
Mousseux Sparkling.
Non-Vintage (NV) A blend of more than one vintage.
Pétillant Faintly sparkling.
Sec Medium-dry.
Vintage A wine of one particular year. Fine champagne vintages: 1985, 1988, 1990, 1995, 1996.

enjoy!

To impress the girls, Napoleon's officers would often slice off the tops of champagne bottles with their sabers, all very well early in the evening when their eye was true…

Notoriously, victorious Formula One drivers spray champagne into the crowds below, such exuberance both depressing the wine-maker and delighting the marketing men. With the pressure inside a bottle of bubbly being about 90 pounds a square inch— roughly the same as the tire pressure needed for a double-decker bus—it is little wonder that the cork pops out so easily, the longest flight of a cork being recorded at 177 feet 9 inches.

Unless you have just won a Grand Prix, the simplest way to open a bottle of bubbly is as follows:

1. Remove the foil and the wire from around the cork.

2. Hold the bottle at an angle, keeping the base in your stronger hand and the cork in the other.

3. Twist the bottle slowly while holding the cork firmly (if you twist the cork, you risk snapping it).

4. Using the pressure inside the bottle to help you, ease the cork out gently. It should come out with a sigh rather than a bang, the noise of which would only draw attention to your enviable drinking habits and make your friends and neighbors jealous.

Bubbly is best served chilled, straight from a cool cellar or after just a couple of hours (rather than days) in the refrigerator. Alternatively, place the bottle inside an ice bucket  filled with a little ice and plenty of water. To pour, grasp the bottle by the base with your thumb inside the indentation. If it is your best bottle, make sure the label points upward so people can see what they are drinking. If it is your worst, make sure it points downward so they can't.

JUST CHILL TO SERVE

Bubbly not only makes an ideal aperitif, it also goes well with caviar, rich pâté, gravadlax, smoked salmon (lox), oysters, or lobster, while sweet bubbly is perfect with sweet soufflés, rich fruit cake, and strawberries and cream. It is also a crucial ingredient of some of the finest and most decadent cocktails, such as:

Bellini: ⅔ bubbly, ⅓ fresh peach juice.

Black Velvet: ½ bubbly, ½ draft Guinness.

Buck's Fizz: ⅔ bubbly, ⅓ fresh orange juice.

Champagne Cocktail: glass of champagne with the addition of a brandy-soaked sugar cube and a dash of Angostura bitters.

Death in the afternoon: ⅚ bubbly ⅙ pernod.

Jojo: ⅔ bubbly, ⅓ fresh strawberry juice.

Kir Royale: 1 glass of bubbly, crème de cassis to taste.

It is better to serve bubbly in "tulips" or "flutes"—elegant glasses that retain the wine's effervescence, as opposed to the shallow "saucers" that allow the sparkle to dissipate far too quickly. For the same reason, it

should be a criminal offense to use a swizzle-stick, an instrument designed to remove the fizz from champagne, thereby undoing the winemaker's painstaking efforts. If you want a still wine, buy a still wine, and leave the bubbles for us!

ENJOY THE BUBBLES!

PICTURE CREDITS

Key: **a**=above, **b**=below, **l**=left, **r**=right
1 photographer Peter Cassidy;
2 photographer Alan Williams;
3-13 photographer Peter Cassidy;
14 photographer Alan Williams;
17 photographer Peter Cassidy;
18 l Ruinart Champagne;
18 r & 19 Champagne Mumm;
21 al photographer Alan Williams;
21 b & r photographer Peter
Cassidy; **22-27** photographer
Peter Cassidy; **28-34 & 35** inset
photographer Alan Williams;
35 main photographer Peter
Cassidy; **36** photographer
Alan Williams; **37 & 38-39**
photographer Peter Cassidy;
40 photographer Alan Williams;
43-64 photographer Peter Cassidy

The publisher and author would like to thank all
the businesses and home owners who assisted
us with the photography for this book.

PLACES TO BUY GLASSES AND OTHER BUBBLY
ACCESSORIES:

ABC CARPET & HOME
888 Broadway
New York, NY 10003
For a store near you, call (212) 473-3000
www.abchome.com

BED, BATH AND BEYOND
620 6th Avenue
New York, NY 10011
For a store near you, call (800) GOBEYOND
www.bedbathandbeyond.com

CRATE & BARREL
1860 W. Jefferson
Naperville, IL 60540
For a store near you, call (800) 967-6696
www.crateandbarrel.com

POTTERY BARN
2488 E. Sunrise Boulevard
Ft. Lauderdale, FL 33304
For a store near you, call (800) 922 9934
www.potterybarn.com

WILLIAMS-SONOMA
51 Highland Park Village
Dallas, TX 75205
For a store near you, call (800) 541-2233
www.williamssonoma.com